The Influence Of William Osler On American Medicine: With A Brief Obituary

George Martin Kober

In the interest of creating a more extensive selection of rare historical book reprints, we have chosen to reproduce this title even though it may possibly have occasional imperfections such as missing and blurred pages, missing text, poor pictures, markings, dark backgrounds and other reproduction issues beyond our control. Because this work is culturally important, we have made it available as a part of our commitment to protecting, preserving and promoting the world's literature. Thank you for your understanding.

With the Compliments of the Author
March 28, 1920

THE INFLUENCE OF DR. WILLIAM OSLER ON AMERICAN MEDICINE

WITH A BRIEF OBITUARY

BY

GEORGE MARTIN KOBER, M.D., LL.D.

PROFESSOR OF HYGIENE AND PREVENTIVE MEDICINE, GEORGETOWN UNIVERSITY
WASHINGTON, D.C.

Reprinted from the Transactions of
The Association of American Physicians
1919

W Osler

THE INFLUENCE OF DR. OSLER ON AMERICAN MEDICINE[1]

By GEORGE M. KOBER, M.D.
WASHINGTON, D. C.

Dr. Osler has passed his seventieth goal post. Sincere personal appreciation of the master work of this chieftain in the art and science of medicine, gratitude for the kindly inspirations experienced through his influence and the sanguine hope that his fair example may stimulate the younger generation to emulate his noble achievements, have prompted the writer to lay the wreath of tribute at the feet of this most deserving of septuagenarians.

Dr. Osler's Early Life and Student Days. William Osler was born in Bond Head, Ontario, July 12, 1849, son of F. L. Osler, clergyman of the Church of England. His were not only rare physical and mental characteristics through parental inheritance, but, as told him by his old and true friend, Dr. Jacobi, at the farewell banquet tendered him on May 2, 1905, "It is no mean felicity to be born with the imprint of virtue."

Those familiar with the portrait of Osler as a school-boy at Trinity College, and those fortunate enough to have been personally associated with him in later years, have read in that face innate qualities which not only endeared him to his friends, but, in the estimate of his dear old mother, "Were more precious than all his honors."

Osler's earliest school life was passed in the school of his native village, following which he went to Port Hope for a term or two in Trinity College School of that place, and later still he entered

---

[1] The portrait of Dr. Osler is printed by courtesy of the American Journal of the Medical Sciences, January, 1920.

Trinity University at Toronto. Devoted to his books during hours of class, he enjoyed his play with the "playful child let loose from school." Robust of health, his mind matured with equal pace.

On quitting Trinity College, young Osler entered the office of Dr. Bovell, at Toronto, as assistant, and there he inaugurated his medical studies, later matriculating in the School of Medicine of McGill University, Montreal, graduating in 1872.

We learn from his classmate, Professor F. J. Shepherd, that while a conscientious worker, Osler never passed for "a grinder." He was not particularly known for his devotion to books, nor were his efforts entirely focussed toward success in examinations, but his main attention was directed toward the postmortem room and to all hospital work within reach. He was beloved because of his social qualities, kindliness of disposition and characteristic sense of humor. Dr. Shepherd remarks: "While he did not graduate very high in his class, there is a note in the convocation that a special prize was awarded for his graduation thesis, because of the originality it displayed and the research it evinced, and because of the collection of pathological specimens accompanying it which were presented to the museum. In the light of his after studies it is interesting to note that some of these specimens, still in the college museum, concerned the ulcers of typhoid fever." As a student, Osler was deeply interested in comparative pathology, and as a teacher in subsequent years, often illustrated a point in human disease by a reference to a parallel condition in the lower animals.

How carefully he prepared himself for the practice of medicine and the professor's chair is evinced in the fact that, following his graduation, he spent two years abroad in study in the laboratory of the physiologist, Burdon-Sanderson, and attending the clinics of Jenner and Wilson Fox, Ringer and Bastian in medicine and the dermatological clinics of Tilbury Fox. In 1873 he took the degree of licentiate of the Royal College of Physicians in London. Thereupon he went to Berlin, where he studied pathology under Virchow, physiological chemistry under Salkowsky, and clinical medicine under Frerichs and Traube. In the early part of 1874 he continued his studies in Vienna under Bamberger, Hebra and other noted clinicians.

DR. OSLER AS A TEACHER AT MCGILL UNIVERSITY. Upon his return to Montreal, in 1874, he was appointed, at the early age of twenty-five, professor of the institutes of medicine at the McGill University, which included the course of physiology and a series of twenty lectures on pathology. In 1875–76 instruction in histology and demonstrations in physiology were added to his work and in the following year a summer course in pathological histology. Dr. Osler served from 1874–1875 as physician to the Smallpox Hospital of Montreal, and it is chronicled that he sacrificed his salary for the purchase of microscopes for his department at the University. Osler, himself, has said that a man should come into internal medicine by one of three ways: Physiological chemistry, physiology or morbid anatomy. He made himself proficient in all three of these branches, especially in pathology.

In the winter of 1875–76 his autopsy work began at the Montreal General Hospital and continued for eight years, with 1000 autopsies to his credit. In 1878 he was appointed physician to this hospital, and there began his career as a brilliant clinical teacher. A man with such firm scientific foundations, a comprehensive knowledge of the subject presented by him, and his personal magnetism could not fail to command the respect and esteem of his students and professional colleagues. He not only awakened interest and enthusiasm in modern scientific medicine among his hearers, but also among the members of the medical societies. Even before the completion of his thirtieth year he figured as a leader, and his influence was felt not only in Canada and the States, but merited for him later the appointment of regius professor of Oxford University. Osler's recollections of his early teaching career are charmingly and modestly set forth in an address delivered at the opening of the session of that school, September 21, 1899, twenty-five years after the faculty, as he declared, "With some hardihood selected a young and untried man to deliver lectures in the institutes of medicine.

"My first appearance before the class filled me with tremulous uneasiness and an overwhelming sense of embarrassment. I shall not forget the nice consideration of my colleagues and the friendly greetings of the boys, which calmed my fluttering heart. One permanent impression abides—the awful task of the preparation of about one hundred lectures. After the ten to twelve with which I started had been exhausted I was on the treadmill for the remainder of the session. False pride forbade the reading of the excellent lectures of my predecessor, Dr. Drake, which with his wonted goodness of heart he had offered. I reached January in an exhausted condition, but relief was at hand. One day the post brought a brand-new book on physiology by a well-known German professor, and it was remarkable with what rapidity my labors of the last half of the session were lightened. An extraordinary improvement in the lectures was noticed, the students benefited and I gained rapidly in the facility with which I could quote the translated German. Four years later I was appointed on the visiting staff of the Montreal General Hospital. What better fortune could a young man desire? I left the same day for London with my dear old friend, George Ross, and the happy days we spent together working at clinical medicine did much to wean me from my first love. From that date I paid more attention to pathology and practical medicine and added to my courses one in morbid anatomy, another in pathological histology and a summer class in clinical medicine. I had become a plurist of the most abandoned sort, and by the end of two years it was difficult to say what I did profess, and I felt like the man to whom Plato applies the words of the poet:

> "'Full many a thing he knew,
> But knew them only badly.'

"Weakened in this way I could not resist when temptation came from pastures new in the fresh and narrower field of clinical medicine. After ten years of hard work I left Montreal a rich man—rich in the treasures of friendship and good fellowship, and those treasures of widened experience and a fuller knowledge of men and manners which contact with the bright minds in the profession necessarily entails. My heart, or a good bit of it at least, has stayed with these treasures."

DR. OSLER IN THE UNIVERSITY OF PENNSYLVANIA. In the summer of 1884 Osler received a call from the University of Pennsylvania. When the invitation to present himself as a candidate for the position of professor of clinical medicine at Philadelphia reached him at Leipzig, Dr. Osler told us he was inclined to believe it a joke. Nor was he disabused of this notion until two weeks later a cablegram reached him to meet Dr. Weir Mitchell in London. He added, with his characteristic humor: "Boston measures men by brains, it is said, New York by baw-bees and Philadelphia by breeding." It was Mitchell's task to test his breeding. He did so by having him eat cherry pie, and noting how he disposed of the stones. As Osler disposed of them discreetly the breeding question was settled.

In 1884 Osler was elected to the Fellowship of the Royal College of Physicians of London and in 1885 was also chosen from the newly elected fellows of the college to deliver the "Gulstonian Lectures," a singular honor which he most efficiently discharged, selecting for his subject "Malignant Endocarditis." His lectures were based on his studies and material available in Montreal. No wonder that a man so highly honored by the Royal College had been chosen the year before to become an associate of Leidy, Pepper, Stillé and other leading lights. Osler's advent in Philadelphia marked a turning-point in the methods of teaching medicine not only in Philadelphia but in the States.

In Philadelphia, as in Montreal, as well said by his friend, Dr. James C. Wilson, he inspired his students with a craving for knowledge based upon facts of the ward, of the miscroscope, of the laboratory, of the postmortem room and also stimulated their interest in medical literature. He demonstrated how medicine should be learned and taught.

He also insisted, with the younger generation, by precept and example, that it is not necessary for every physician to be a practitioner in the ordinary sense, but that long years of hospital and laboratory work constitute a better equipment for the teacher and consultant.

DR. OSLER AT JOHNS HOPKINS MEDICAL SCHOOL. In 1889, at the age of forty, Osler was invited to Baltimore to take charge of the medical clinic of the Johns Hopkins Hospital. From this time out dates clearly his greatest activity and usefulness in professional work.

Professor William H. Welch advises us that when Dr. Osler came to Baltimore the main intention of the faculty was that the hospital should form an integral part of the medical school and that opportunities should be afforded for higher clinical training. It accordingly seemed expedient that students should be made part of the hospital machinery, and to Osler is due the credit of working out the details of the scheme. This, indeed, represents his contribution to medical teaching in America.

As in Philadelphia so in Baltimore, Osler's impression on the local profession was profound. The following tribute, found in the *Maryland Medical Journal* for June, 1905, attests this: "He has taught them the value of work for the sake of work; he has shown them the beauty of labor; he has been to them an ever-present example of right living and right thinking; he has shown by word and example the duty the physician owes his patient, his brother in the medical fraternity and the community at large; he has broadened the scope of the physician's calling and he has shown him that the good man and the good citizen must both be present to make the good physician possible."

DR. OSLER'S INFLUENCE ON HIGHER MEDICAL EDUCATION. Over forty published essays and addresses bearing on medical education and medical history are sufficient warrant of Osler's keen interest in this subject.

He was ever a staunch advocate of higher premedical education requirements, extension of the period of professional study and the substitution of laboratory instruction for didactic teaching. In his "Essay on the Need of Radical Reforms in the Methods of Teaching Senior Students," he advises teachers "to give to students an education of such a character that they can become sensible practitioners."

Dr. Osler was convinced that it is the duty of a medical school to see that the senior student "begins his studies with the patient, continues them with the patient, ends them with the patient, using books and lectures as tools, means to an end."

He persistently maintained that the ideal hospital is one connected with a medical school, with the professors members of the attending staff. In this connection he writes: "The work of an institution in which there is no teaching is rarely first class. It is, I think, safe to say that in a hospital with students in the wards the patients are more carefully looked after, their diseases are more fully studied and fewer mistakes are made."

Osler's methods of teaching clinical medicine fitted in admirably with the general policy of the faculty that the students should be made a part of the machinery of the hospital. As a result the clinical unit was maintained in the fourth year as taught by him, but the work transferred from the out-patient department to the wards. In Osler's judgment "each man should be allowed to serve for at least half of the session in the medical wards and half in the surgical wards. He should be assigned four or five beds, and under the supervision of the house physician he does all the work in connection with his own patients. One or two of the clinical units are taken around the wards three or four times a week by one of the teachers for a couple of hours, the cases commented upon, the students asked questions and the group made familiar with the progress of the cases. In this way the student gets a familiarity with disease, a practical knowledge of clinical medicine and a practical knowledge of how to treat disease."

Though Dr. Osler disclaims any credit for his teaching method, it is nevertheless unquestionable that had it not been for his wonderful personality, enthusiastic and effective leadership, American medical education might still be fifty years in arrear of that of Europe. It required a man of his broad vision, sound judgment, a devotee to his profession and a statesman in medicine to make converts to the cause of his revolutionary ideals. Dr. Arnold Klebs has deeded us in Garrison's history an admirable pen portrait of the doctor as clinical professor at the Johns Hopkins Hospital:

"Never can one forget the scenes in the out-patient department, where he stood surrounded by his boys, helping them as a friend in their struggles with some difficult case. He would go to one, put his arm around his shoulder and then begin a friendly inquiry, interspersed with humorous remarks and allusions to the work done by special students on a given subject. Urging, encouraging, inspiring, so we saw him always exact, dogmatic never, and when the humorous, friendly fire kindled in his eyes we could not help but love him, and with him the task we had chosen for our life work."

We feel that we would be omitting an important page in the story of Osler's activities were we to pass over in silence those homely Saturday evening gatherings, held at the table round in his magnificent library, where he offered what Garrison characterizes as "the best models of charming essays on medical history," and estimated by Sudhoff "to contain more of the historical spirit than many learned works of the professional historian. The reason is that Osler loves his old authors as he does his profession."

These gatherings also enabled him to familiarize himself with the individuality of each student and in his charming way to offer timely and valuable suggestions as to how to solve certain intellectual and moral problems. Johns Hopkins Medical School has become known as the mother of medical teachers, and since 213 of the 453 graduates who were also his pupils prior to 1906, are or have been connected with our medical schools, it is easy to infer the extent of his beneficent influence.

Dr. Osler realizing, as every master mind necessarily must, the value of example, ever inculcated on his student body esteem for the general practitioner and old-style country doctor. Most of his pupils will cherish gratefully the words addressed to them during class hours: "Many of you have been influenced in your choice of a profession by the example and friendship for the old family doctor or of some country practitioner in whom you have recognized the highest type of mankind and whose unique position in the community has filled you with laudable ambition. You will do well to make such a man your example, and I would urge you to start with no higher ambition than to join the noble band of general practitioners. They form the very sinews of the profession—generous-hearted men, with well-balanced, cool heads, not scientific always, but learned in the wisdom of the sick room if not in the laboratories."

Osler was deeply interested in the progress of American medicine and proud of its achievements, as shown in his address delivered at the opening of the Museum of the Medical Graduates' College and Polyclinic in London on July 4, 1900, in which he pointed out the silent revolution which had taken place in medical education, and especially in the cultivation of the scientific branches, hospital equipment and clinical facilities:

"The most hopeful feature is a restless discontent which, let us hope, may not be allayed until the revolution is complete in all respects. Meantime, to students who wish to have the best that the world offers, let me suggest that the lines of intellectual progress are veering strongly to the West, and I predict that in the twentieth century the young English physicians will find their keenest inspiration in the land of the setting sun."

It is quite natural that a man with such high hopes and aspirations would strongly resent any interference with the legitimate and humane methods employed for the advancement of scientific medicine.

I shall never forget the expression of scorn in his eyes and the words with which he rebuked the enemies of scientific progress, who had been heard before the United States Senate Committee on a bill for the further prevention of cruelty to animals: "The blood just surged in my veins, Sir, when I heard two men address you today, say things which they should have been ashamed to say of the medical profession, of men who daily give their lives for their fellows. . . . With reference to men who train with these enemies of the profession, I say this, that I scorn them from my heart." (See Hearing on Vivisection, February 21, 1900, Government Printing Office, Washington.) The bill failed in the committee and no serious attempt has been made to enact what Osler characterized as "a piece of unnecessary legislation."[1]

DR. OSLER'S INFLUENCE ON THE PROFESSION AT LARGE. The many invitations extended and accepted by Dr. Osler to address medical societies attest the savory, widespread influence his career wielded over the medical community at home and abroad. His text-book, *Principles and Practice of Medicine*, graces the bookshelves of well-nigh every English-speaking physician the world over.

[1] Since the above was written a bill known as S. 1258, to prohibit experiments upon living dogs in the District of Columbia, was introduced and hearings were held before the Subcommittee of the Committee on the Judiciary, U. S. Senate, November 1, 1919, and it is hoped that the bill will not be enacted.

The medical societies, the efficient vehicle, as he took it, for the dissemination of scholarship, ever received his heartiest encouragement. Accordingly, we find him either enrolled as an active member of these societies or fostering their foundation, because, as he said, to the members and friends on the occasion of the centennial celebration of the New Haven Medical Association, January 6, 1903: "The society is a school in which the scholars teach each other, and there is no better way than by the demonstration of the more unusual cases that happen to fall in your way." Through these societies he awakened interest in postmortem work, the presentation of pathological specimens and in library equipment. Through them, also, he emphasized what a well-equipped and properly manned hospital in every town of 50,000 inhabitants could effect toward the advancement of clinical medicine. Through them he felt that America would accomplish more for clinical medicine in five years than Germany could in ten.

Osler was one of the most active founders of the Association of American Physicians, organized at a meeting held in the office of Dr. Francis Delafield, New York City, October 10, 1885. Others present at this time were Drs. William H. Draper, William Pepper, James Tyson, George L. Peabody and Robert T. Edes.

The first scientific meeting of the Association was convened in Washington, June 17, 1886, and from that meeting until his departure for Oxford he was recorded absent from the meetings but twice. Even after his departure he attended several meetings, and was elected an honorary member in 1912. In 1894 he was elected president of the Association, and in his address delivered May 30, 1895, he spoke in part as follows:

"At the opening of our tenth meeting the question is timely—How far has the Association fulfilled the object it had in view? Have our aspirations and hopes of 1885 been realized? We sought, as stated in Article I of our Constitution, the advancement of scientific and practical medicine. With this primary object we sought also, as Dr. Delafield said in his opening remarks, an association in which there will be no medical politics and no medical ethics; an association in which no one will care who are the officers and who are not; in which we will not ask from which part of the country a man comes, but whether he had done good work, and will do more, whether he has anything to say worth saying and can say it."

Osler believed that the nine volumes of the *Transactions* offered a full and satisfactory answer to the first question and referred to them as "the repository of very much that is best in American medical literature." He emphasized the widespread and effective interest which the papers of Dr. Fitz on "Appendicitis" and of Dr. F. M. Draper on "Pancreatic Hemorrhage" had produced, and succinctly reviewed some of the topics presented for discussion, such as typhoid fever, the parasites of malaria, tuberculosis, diseases of the gastric intestinal tract, diseases of the heart, blood, bloodvessels, kidneys, etc. He boldly stated that several papers had been presented which indicated that the readers had failed to grasp the scope of the Association. He declared that the Association had already shown a powerful influence on the study of pathological and clinical medicine in this country, that there was at present an actual scarcity of trained pathologists and bacteriologists and a distinct need of well-trained special clinical physicians, and of such physicians and of pathologists and bacteriologists should the Association in greater part be composed.

He referred to the limited membership, and with characteristic frankness declared: "We should all understand that this is a working society, and when any one of us ceases to attend regularly, or when our interest grows lukewarm, we will promote best the common welfare by quickly retiring."[1]

Osler was a member of the Council of the Association for a number of years and exercised a strict but just censorship over the admission of members; he was doubtless the most active and fruitful worker in that body, as shown by ten original contributions and his discussion of sixty-four papers presented by other members. He was as popular among his colleagues in the Association as a teacher as with his classes in the medical school. The young and the old were attracted, inspired and improved, and men like Jacobi and

---

[1] The membership of the Association in 1886 was limited to 100, which was increased in 1897 to 125, in 1904 to 135 active and 25 associate members and further increased to 1912 to 160 active and 25 associate members. Active members after ten years' service may be transferred to the list of emeritus members. Honorary membership is limited to 25.

others much older than he have told him that they were glad to sit at his feet and listen to him. Since the majority of these men were occupying professorial chairs the sphere of his beneficent influence has been greatly evidenced. He was also an enthusiastic founder of the National Association for the Study and Prevention of Tuberculosis in 1904, and has been the Honorary Vice-President ever since 1905.

When Osler, well-nigh fifty years ago, stood upon the threshold of his professional life, he stood there convinced of the dignity and responsibilities of his lofty avocation. He stood there convinced that if his name were to be dug deep in the marble walls of the hall of fame, it had to be dug therein with the chisels of study, honesty and truth. He has now lived a lifetime of life and lived it well. He has lived a lifetime of study as evinced by over seven hundred and thirty contributions to medical literature. He has lived a lifetime of service to his fellowman, to which bear witness his contributions to preventive medicine, his active participation in the eradication of preventable disease, his kindly ministrations to the sick poor. He has lived a lifetime which has been an honor to his profession and a glory to his professional brethren. A lifetime which has been rewarded with every honor and trust at home and abroad which the medical community could possibly bestow upon him. He has lived a lifetime of service, and during this lifetime he has tempered tenderness with firmness, condescension with authority. His only protest against cares was silence. Dignity met his responsibilities; equanimity his successes and griefs, sufferings and disappointments. And as our congratulations go out to him there follows the sincere hope that his days of activity and bliss may still be many to complement this lifetime that shall know no death.

Unfortunately the universal hope of Sir William Osler's friends that he might live long to enjoy the evening of his life has not been realized. It is, however, a comforting reflection that his life, so full of honors, was spared until after he attained the scriptural age of three score and ten. In the last year of his life he had the satisfaction of being elected to the presidency of the British Classical Association, "a singular and much appreciated honor for a medical man." An honor more highly cherished by him was the international celebration of his seventieth birthday, when on July 12 he received the felicitations and congratulations of the medical world and the Anniversary Volumes prepared by his students and colleagues.

In response to the presentation address, Dr. Osler said:

"To have had the benediction of friendship follow one like a shadow, to have always had the sense of comradeship in work, without the petty pinpricks of jealousies and controversies, to be able to rehearse in the sessions of sweet, silent thought the experiences of long years without a single bitter memory, fill the heart with gratitude. That three transplantations have been borne successfully is a witness to the brotherly care with which you have tended me. Loving our profession, and believing ardently in its future, I have been content to live in it and for it. A moving ambition to become a good teacher and a sound clinician was fostered by opportunities of an exceptional character, and any success I may have attained must be attributed in large part to the unceasing kindness of colleagues and to a long series of devoted pupils whose success in life is my special pride."

The writer cannot help but feel that the days of our beloved chief, like those of many other men and mothers, with courageous but sympathetic hearts, have been shortened by the cruel world war. He lost his only son and also a nephew on the western battle fields, and his silent but intense grief, combined with overwork, did much to undermine his constitution.

The first information of his impaired health reached me in a card dated November 19, in which he wrote: "I have been laid up for some weeks with bronchitis, but am better now." Pneumonia developed and later pleurisy, with effusion, necessitating a thoracentesis. On Christmas Day he sent a cheerful, hopeful telegram to his friends at the Johns Hopkins Hospital, that he was making a good fight, but on December 29 came the end, at his home in Norham Gardens, which was felt as a shock throughout the English-speaking world. He has gone to his long home. Minerva Medica has ushered him through the portals beyond and proudly but reverently presented him to the Supreme Healer of the Universe as a type of the true physician, whose spirit will abide with us now and always!

Printed by Libri Plureos GmbH in Hamburg, Germany